D0306548

ABBEY THEATRE ON TOUR
TERMINUS
MARK O'ROWE

Terminus premiered at the Abbey Theatre on the Peacock stage in June 2007. It also toured in 2008 and 2009. The current 2011 production is touring internationally.

The Abbey Theatre gratefully acknowledges the financial support of the Arts Council / An Chomhairle Ealaíon.

This production runs without an interval

CAST *(in order of appearance)*

A	Olwen Fouéré
B	Catherine Walker
C	Declan Conlon

Director	Mark O'Rowe
Set and Costume Design	Jon Bausor
Lighting Design	Philip Gladwell
Sound Design	Philip Stewart
Stage Manager	Stephanie Ryan
Production Manager	Des Kenny
Production Electrician (UK Tour)	Dave Carpenter

Terminus by Mark O'Rowe is an Abbey Theatre commission.

Terminus is part of our published playscript series.
For further titles in the series please visit www.abbeytheatre.ie

*Special thanks to Wayne Jordan, Andrew Bennett, Derbhle Crotty
and Mary Murray.*

...

TERMINUS
MARK O'ROWE

ABBEY THEATRE
Amharclann na Mainistreach

The **Abbey Theatre,** Ireland's national theatre was founded by W.B Yeats and Lady Gregory in 1904 to 'bring upon the stage the deeper thoughts and emotions of Ireland'. Since it first opened its doors, the Abbey Theatre has played a vital and often controversial role in the literary, social and cultural life of Ireland.

Over the years, the Abbey Theatre has nurtured and premiered the work of major playwrights such as J.M. Synge and Sean O'Casey as well as contemporary classics from the likes of Sebastian Barry, Marina Carr, Bernard Farrell, Brian Friel, Frank McGuinness, Thomas Kilroy, Tom Mac Intyre, Tom Murphy, Mark O'Rowe, Billy Roche and Sam Shepard. We continue to support new Irish writing at the Abbey through our commissioning process and our New Playwrights Programme.

The Abbey produces an annual programme of diverse, engaging, innovative Irish and international theatre. We place the writer and theatre-maker at the heart of all that we do, commissioning and producing exciting new work and creating discourse and debate on the political, cultural and social issues of the day. We connect with a new generation of theatre-goers through our Engage and Learn activities and through our popular Abbey Talks series.

In 1911 the Abbey Theatre first toured internationally. With a world-class reputation, the Abbey Theatre continues to tour taking on the role of an ambassador for Irish arts and culture worldwide.

Annie Horniman provided crucial financial support to the Abbey in its first years and many others have followed her lead by investing in and supporting our work. Now more than ever, we need support to ensure we continue to fuel the flame our founders lit over a century ago.

W.B. Yeats agus an Bantiarna Augusta Gregory a bhunaigh Amharclann na Mainistreach, amharclann náisiúnta na hÉireann, i 1904, d'fhonn na smaointe agus na mothúcháin ba dhoimhne de chuid na hÉireann a láithriú ar an stáitse. Riamh anall ón uair a d'oscail sí a doirse den chéad uair, bhí, agus tá, ról ríthábhachtach agus go deimhin, ról a bhí sách conspóideach go minic, ag Amharclann na Mainistreach i saol liteartha, sóisialta agus cultúrtha na hÉireann.

In imeacht na mblianta, rinne Amharclann na Mainistreach saothar mórdhrámadóirí ar nós J.M. Synge agus Sean O'Casey a chothú agus a chéadléiriú, mar a rinne sí freisin i gcás clasaicigh chomhaimseartha ó dhrámadóirí amhail Sebastian Barry, Marina Carr, Bernard Farrell, Brian Friel, Frank McGuinness, Thomas Kilroy, Tom Mac Intyre, Tom Murphy, Mark O'Rowe, Billy Roche agus Sam Shepard. Leanaimid de thacaíocht a thabhairt do nuasríbhneoireacht na hÉireann in Amharclann na Mainistreach trínár bpróiseas coimisiúnúcháin agus ár gClár do Dhrámadóirí Nua.

Léiríonn Amharclann na Mainistreach clár amharclannaíochta as Éirinn agus ó thíortha thar lear in aghaidh na bliana atá ilghnéitheach, tarraingteach agus nuálach. Cuirimid an scríbhneoir agus an t-amharclannóir i gcroílár an uile ní a dhéanaimid, agus saothar nua spreagúil á choimisiúnú agus á léiriú againn agus dioscúrsa agus díospóireacht á chruthú i dtaobh cheisteanna polaitiúla, cultúrtha agus sóisialta na linne. Cruthaímid nasc leis an nglúin nua gnáthóirí amharclainne trínar ngníomhaíochtaí 'Téigh i ngleic leis agus Foghlaim' agus tríd an tsraith Cainteanna dár gcuid a bhfuil an-tóir orthu.

I 1911 is ea a chuaigh complacht Amharclann na Mainistreach ar camchuairt idirnáisiúnta den chéad uair. Anois, agus cáil dhomhanda uirthi, leanann Amharclann na Mainistreach uirthi i mbun camchuairte agus í ina hambasadóir ar fud an domhain d'ealaíona agus cultúr na hÉireann.

Sholáthair Annie Horniman tacaíocht airgid ríthábhachtach don Mhainistir siar i mblianta tosaigh na hamharclainne agus lean iliomad daoine eile an dea-shampla ceannródaíochta sin uaithi ó shin trí infheistíocht a dhéanamh inár gcuid oibre agus tacaíocht a thabhairt dúinn. Anois thar aon am eile, tá tacaíocht ag teastáil uainn lena chinntiú go leanfaimid den lóchrann sin a d'adhain ár mbunaitheoirí breis agus céad bliain ó shin a choinneáil ar lasadh.

Creative Team & Cast

MARK O'ROWE

WRITER AND DIRECTOR

MARK O'ROWE'S plays include *Terminus* (Abbey Theatre, 2007), *From Both Hips* (Fishamble, 1997), *Anna's Ankle* (Bedrock, 1997), *Howie the Rookie* (Bush, 1999), *Made in China* (Abbey, 2001) and *Crestfall* (Gate Theatre, 2003). Screenplays include *Intermission* (Company of Wolves, 2004), *Boy A* (Channel 4, 2007) based on the novel by Jonathan Trigell, and *Perrier's Bounty* (Parallel, 2009).

JON BAUSOR

SET AND COSTUME DESIGN

JON'S WORK at the Abbey Theatre includes *Big Love, Romeo and Juliet* and *Julius Caesar*. He has designed extensively in theatre, opera and dance for companies including the Royal National Theatre, Royal Opera House, Royal Shakespeare Company, Royal Court and Finnish National Opera. Recent theatre work includes *Ghost Stories* (Liverpool Playhouse / Duke of Yorks, West End), KURSK, shortlisted Best Design Evening Standard awards (Sound and Fury / Young Vic), *King Lear* and *The Winter's Tale* (RSC). *King Lear* will open the new Royal Shakespeare Theatre in Stratford following transfers with *The Winter's Tale* going to London's Roundhouse and the Armoury in New York. In 2006 Jon visited Baghdad to design the Old Vic's production of *The Soldier's Tale*, and more recently Palestine to design *I am Yusuf and this is my brother* for the theatre company Shebbahurr in association with the Young Vic Theatre and Bouffes du Nord, Paris. Other theatre design includes *The Birthday Party* (Lyric Hammersmith), *Water* (Filter / Lyric), *No Wise Men*, winner Best Design Liverpool Daily Post (Peepolykus / Liverpool Playhouse), *James and the Giant Peach*, nominated Best Design Manchester Evening News Awards (Octagon, Bolton), *Scenes from the Back of Beyond* (Royal Court), *Sanctuary* and *The Tempest* (National Theatre, London). Opera design includes *The Knot Garden* (Theatre an der Wien, Vienna), *Queen of Spades* (Edinburgh Festival Theatre), *The Lighthouse* (Teatro Poliziano, Montepulciano) and *The Human Comedy* (Young Vic). Design for dance includes *Blood Wedding* (Finnish National Ballet), *Pleasure's Progress, Ghosts, Before the Tempest* (Royal Opera House), *A Tale of Two Cities* (Northern Ballet Theatre), *Scribblings* (Rambert), *Firebird, HOWL* (Bern Ballet, Switzerland), *Snow White in Black* (Phoenix Dance Theatre) and

Mixtures (English National Ballet). Jon is currently designing *Silence* (RSC / Filter) and *Lord of the Flies* (Regents Park). He trained on the Motley Theatre Design course after studying Music as a choral scholar at Oxford University.

PHILIP GLADWELL

LIGHTING DESIGN

PHILIP'S THEATRE WORK includes *Love The Sinner* (National Theatre, London), *Miss Julie* (Schaubuehne, Berlin), *Five Guys Named Moe* (Underbelly / Theatre Royal Stratford East), *Punk Rock* (Lyric, national tour), *The Duchess of Malfi* (Royal Theatre, Northampton), *Mogadishu, Nineteen Eighty-Four, Macbeth* (Manchester Royal Exchange), *The King And I* (Curve Theatre Leicester), *My Romantic History* (Bush / Sheffield / Fringe First Edinburgh), *Small Hours* (Hampstead Theatre), *The Fahrenheit Twins* (Told by an Idiot), *Origins* (Pentabus), *Once on This Island* (Birmingham Rep / Nottingham Playhouse / Hackney Empire), *I ought to be in Pictures* (Library Manchester), *Harvest* (UK tour), *Amazonia, Ghosts, The Member of the Wedding, Festa!* (Young Vic), *Oxford Street, Kebab* (Royal Court), *Testing the Echo* (Out of Joint), *Daisy Pulls it Off, Blithe Spirit, Black Comedy* (The Watermill), *Low Pay? Don't Pay!, Drowning On Dry Land* (Salisbury Playhouse), *Dandy in the Underworld, Shradda, Overspill, HOTBOI, Tape* (Soho Theatre), *Melody, In the Bag* (Traverse), *Mother Courage and Her Children* (Nottingham Playhouse / UK tour), *Inheritance, The Bodies* (Live Theatre) and *Bread and Butter* (Tricycle). Opera and ballet credits include *After Dido* (English National Opera), *Cosi Fan Tutte* (Welsh National Opera), *Another America, Fire, Awakening* (Sadler's Wells), *Il trittico* (Opera Zuid), *Falstaff* (Grange Park Opera), *Oedipus Rex* (Royal Festival Hall) and *The Canterville Ghost* (Peacock).

PHILIP STEWART

SOUND DESIGN

PHILIP'S WORK at the Abbey Theatre includes *Macbeth, Ages of the Moon, Lay Me Down Softly, A Number* and *The Big House.* As a freelance composer he has contributed music to a broad spectrum of genres including theatre, dance, documentaries and short films. Philip studied composition at Trinity College Dublin under Donnacha Dennehy and Roger Doyle.

DECLAN CONLON
c

DECLAN WAS MOST recently seen at the Abbey Theatre as Peter in Tom Murphy's new play *The Last Days of a Reluctant Tyrant*. Other performances of Tom Murphy's work at the Abbey include Micheal in *A Whistle in the Dark*, Mickelen O'Leary in *Famine* and *The Patriot Game*. Other performances at the Abbey include Creon in Seamus Heaney's *The Burial at Thebes*, John Proctor in *The Crucible*, Captain Plume in *The Recruiting Officer*, Brutus in *Julius Caesar*, Micheal in Brian Friel's adaptation of Turgenev's *A Month in The Country* (Best Supporting Actor, Irish Times Theatre Awards), Lee in Sam Shepard's *True West*, Polonius in *The Hamlet Project*, Chris in *All My Sons*, Hotspur in *Henry IV Part 1*, Stuart Parker's *Heavenly Bodies* and *What Happened Bridgie Cleary*. Appearances at the Gate Theatre, Dublin include a one man adaptation of John Banville's *The Book of Evidence* (originally produced in conjunction with Kilkenny Arts Festival) and Jack in *The Importance of Being Earnest*. Work for the Royal Shakespeare Company includes *As You Like It*, *The Spanish Tragedy*, *La Lupa*, *The Mysteries* and *Henry VI*. At the National Theatre, London, Declan appeared in *The Walls*, *The Ends of the Earth* and *The Machine Wreckers*. Other UK theatre credits include Macduff in *Macbeth* (West End) and *Our Country's Good* for Out of Joint at the Young Vic. Performances for other Irish Theatre companies include Francisco in *The Sanctuary Lamp* directed by Tom Murphy for b*spoke theatre company, *Improbable Frequency* and *Copenhagen* (Nominated Best Actor, Irish times Theatre Awards) for Rough Magic, Jean in *Miss Julie* (Landmark productions) and Martin Crimp's *The Country* (Arclight). Television includes Mendoza in *The Tudors* (Showtime), *Single-Handed* (RTÉ / ITV), *Raw*, *Trouble in Paradise*, *Proof*, *Bachelors Walk* (RTÉ), *Any Time Now*, *Dangerfield*, *The Family* (BBC) and *Cromwell* (Title Films). Films include *Hereafter* directed by Clint Eastwood, *Trouble with Sex*, *Honest* and *All Souls Day*. Radio includes Creon in Seamus Heaney's *The Burial at Thebes* and *The Hounds of the Baskerville*.

OLWEN FOUÉRÉ

ᴀ

OLWEN HAS played several major roles at the Abbey Theatre including Woman in *Woman and Scarecrow*, Hester Swane in the world premiere of *By the Bog of Cats* and the title role in *The Mai*, all by Marina Carr and Ness in *A Cry from Heaven* by Vincent Woods, directed by Olivier Py. She has performed extensively in Ireland and the UK, touring internationally and playing leading roles in numerous productions with the Gate Theatre, Dublin, the National Theatre, London, the Royal Shakespeare Company and in the West End. Other international appearances of note include *Life is a Dream* directed by Calixto Bieito (Edinburgh International Festival, Barbican and BAM) and the title role in the original Gate Theatre production of *Salomé* directed by Steven Berkoff. She was an Artistic Director of Operating Theatre (1980 – 2008) which she co-founded and has recently established a new artistic entity called *TheEmergencyRoom*. Recent stage appearances include *The Rehearsal-Playing the Dane* (Pan Pan theatre), *Yellow RePerfomed* by Amanda Coogan, *Medea* (Siren productions), Celle de Sodome in the world premiere of Laurent

Gaudé's *Sodome My Love* which she translated and for which she received an Irish Times Theatre Award for Best Actress (Rough Magic /*TheEmergencyRoom* at Project Arts Centre, Dublin and Ohrid Festival, Macedonia), The Cailleach in *The Rite of Spring* (Fabulous Beast and the English National Opera at the London Coliseum) and *Under Glass* with the Clod Ensemble commissioned by Sadler's Wells. Other recent appearances include her solo performance in the French stage adaptation of two books by Roddy Doyle, *Paula Spencer, la femme qui se cognait dans le portes* which toured France and played at the Bouffes du Nord, Paris and Maeve in *The Bull* (Fabulous Beast, Dublin Theatre Festival and the Barbican) which was nominated for two Olivier Awards. Recent films include *This Must be the Place* with Sean Penn directed by Paolo Sorrentino, *The Rafters* directed by John Carney and *The Other Side of Sleep* directed by Rebecca Daly. A documentary film of a year in Olwen's life *Theatre in the Flesh* was made in 2004, directed by Dara McCluskey.

CATHERINE WALKER

CATHERINE'S LAST appearance at the Abbey Theatre was in *What Happened Bridgie Cleary* for which she won an Irish Times Theatre Award for Best Actress. She also performed the title role in *Phaedra* (Dublin Theatre Festival), La Presidente de Tourvel in *Les Liaisons Dangereuses*, Yelena in *Uncle Vanya* (Gate Theatre), *Play* for the Beckett Centenary Festival (Gate Theatre and Barbican, London), the title role in *Miss Julie, Blackbird, Knives in Hens* (Landmark) and Marina Carr's *The Giant Blue Hand* (The Ark). Work for the Royal Shakespeare Company includes Katherine in *Henry V*, Vera in *A Month in the Country, Troilus and Cressida* and *Richard II*. Other work includes Olivia in *Twelfth Night* (English Touring Theatre), *John Bull's Other Island*, the title role in *Sive* (Tricycle Theatre), *Wild Orchids* (Chichester Festival Theatre), Tennessee Williams' *Stairs to the Roof* (Minerva Theatre, Chichester), *Blackwater Angel* (Finborough Theatre), Cordelia in *King Lear* (Second Age) and *Diary of a New York Lady* (Samuel Beckett Centre). Television credits include *The Silence* (BBC), Eleanor Tilney in *Northanger Abbey* (Granada / ITV), *The Clinic* (RTÉ), *Lewis* (ITV), *Waking the Dead* (BBC), *Animals,* (Channel 4), *Cromwell in Ireland* (Title Films), *Perfect Day* (Channel 5) and *Bittersweet* (RTÉ). Films include *The Other Side, Leap Year, Passenger on Board, Conspiracy of Silence, Easier Ways to Make a Living* and *Sweeney Todd.*

NO ROMANCE
NANCY HARRIS

THE PASSING
PAUL MERCIER

THE EAST PIER
PAUL MERCIER

PERVE
STACEY GREGG

NEW WRITING AT THE ABBEY

www.abbeytheatre.ie

TERMINUS

Mark O'Rowe

For Aoife

4

Characters

A   *female, forties*

B   *female, twenties*

C   *male, thirties*

This text went to press before the end of rehearsals and so may differ slightly from the play as performed.

Lights up on A, B *and* C. *Hold. Lights down on* B *and* C.

A

'This Samaritan shit's the pits,' I think, as I try to talk a guy
from the brink of suicide; a gun implied at first, then at last
admitted to. A bullet through the head his plan.

Now, I should be calm, it goes without saying; but instead I'm
filled with distress as I stupidly ask his name, his address, then
dread as I hear a shot, then not any more as I hear him say, 'Got
you, you gullible whore!' and hang up with a snigger, the
fucking fake!

I figure I'll duck outside for a break, and do, have a suck on a
cigarette and rue my volunteering for this, fearing I don't have
the sand, the grit, the bit of detachment required – Ah, shit –
Sure, mired as I am in sympathy, you see, what possible help
can I be to these loveless lost, what cost to them my hapless,
helpless, hopeless best, my messed-up endeavours?

And so, I confess, I consider just quitting this shit altogether
and splitting home right away. However, my duty decrees that I
stay till the end of my shift, which is only fair, I guess. So,
until nine, it's back to my chair, my desk, my phone, to take
more calls, which come as a stream of imprecations, hopeless
tales and despairing petitions until a petition in particular gives
me pause, or rather the voice which imparts it, because it's a
voice I'm certain I recollect, someone I taught in school, I
suspect, then am sure of. Yes. A girl called Helen I had for
maths. A fucking mess. Though that's a tale best told at a better
time. For now, she's saying she needs an abortion. Fine. I ask
her how many months she's gone, she says, 'Nine.' I say,
'What?!' She says, 'Sorry. Eight.' I say, 'Jesus, either way,
that's way too late. Now, look: a baby doesn't have to be the

end, you know? And, understand, there are people you can go to who…' And here she screams so loud my eardrum seems to perforate, and in the calm that follows calmly states that whether I help or not, it's happening. 'What?' I say. 'Helen?! What does that mean?!' She hesitates having heard her name, then – click! – the line goes dead.

She's gone.

And I feel sick for not having been adept or slick enough to have kept her on, and annoyed at myself as I am, I decide to leave after all, and to hell with my duty, my fucking shift, I'm out of here and drifting now toward the nearest pub in order to clear my head, to have a mull.

When I get inside the place is full, but, moving through the mill, I discover a table being cleared by a waiter, off whom I order a vodka and water, then, taking a seat and receiving my drink, I allow myself to really think about Helen's call, her request, her appalling tone and intention…

Did I mention, by the way, that she was a student of mine when I taught? Okay. But did I also say that there was a time when I ought to have helped her, but hadn't? I didn't. Many a time in fact, her being the kind of girl who attracted derision, incited spite, who was constantly picked on, the other kids delighting in seeing her suffer. Why? Who knows? I mean, there are those, I'll grant, who just give off that particular scent, but the sudden fit of guilt I feel since her call, the shame, for never having intervened at the time, combined with the fact it was me she got back there tonight, my line, is beginning to feel like a sign, a dare, or a command, to find her, and I understand if you deem this kind of reasoning extreme, but I've always been a woman who'll embrace her intuition and obey it, and today it's saying, Save this girl, you know? Protect her.

And so, having sunk a second drink, then a third, and by now sufficiently inspired, I step outside and stride again, my destination home, to carry out stage one of my plan: a climb to the attic, a comb through files, two piles worth of student details, addresses, and, yes, it's here, what I guess is my only

lead: the home of her mother. I write it down, then make my
way there, knock on the door twenty minutes later.

The mother answers.

'Hey there,' I say, and tell her I taught her daughter, Helen, way
back when and, since I was in the vicinity, thought I might drop
in for a minute, just to see how she's getting on. Far-fetched, I
know, but the woman plays along, turning and making a gesture
to follow, so I do. She's thin, eyes hollow. Suppose she's a
drinker – the state of the place, the funk! – or a junkie.

We sit, she smokes, a kitten in the corner pokes at an empty
tuna tin. We watch it a minute, then she begins: 'Helen's dead to
me, love,' she says.

I ask why.

'For getting knocked up by some guy for one; for getting a taste
for cunny, two.'

'For what?!'

'Honey, *you* know what they're like, those dirty dykes, the
things they do. And, three, because she called me a junkie
whore; and four, because I'm no more that than a lover of
smelly gat like her and that fucking pig's behind, Celine
O'Brien, the bitch who bent her,' she says, 'sent her lez, and
made her a concubine in her filthy dirty dyke harem.'

Seconds pass as I try to process this. Then I ask for this Celine's
address.

She chokes a bit, says, 'You're joking! Shit, that crazy bitch, if
she feels it befits you will fucking blitz you, break you to bits,
you even look at her crooked. Fuck that shit.'

And she stares at the cat.

But there's no way I'm gonna leave it at that, so I ask again and,
shaking her head, she takes out a pen, says, 'Fair enough. It's
your life, man,' and scribbles it down, then turns away as if to
say, 'Now, go,' and so, I take what she's written, thank her, pet
the kitten, withdraw from the kitchen, the hall, the house, and

wander, wondering whether she's really that mean, this Celine, that fearsome, and if it'd make more sense to veer somewhat to the left; a lot, in fact; a full one hundred and eighty degrees, and just turn back. Give up. Go home.

But, God, how can I when it's me alone who can help this child? So, instead, I roam a while until I find a cab to nab and get in and we go, the driver prattling on the way they do. I couldn't be bothered responding. I tune him out and drift and, miffed at my lack of response to his shit, he quits his attempts to engage and sits in a childish rage till we're there and, having paid my fare and got out, I hear, as he pulls away, him say, or rather grunt, 'You ignorant cunt!' and, unfazed by his curse – I know, I know. But I've been called worse – I go to the gate and enter, knock and wait on tenterhooks till she answers the door.

Celine.

There's no doubt that it's her. I mean, 'pig's behind' might be going too far, but not much. And as she comes near, such a fearsome blast of breath takes mine away, combined with a spray of spit which hits me right on the cheek when she speaks, says, 'What?'

'Is Helen there?'

'She's not,' she says.

'Do you know where she is?'

'I do,' she says, coming closer. 'Why the fuck are you looking for her?' To which I reply, to my absolute horror, 'It's none of your business,' and something whizzes toward my eye – her fucking fist! – and lands with a sizeable thwack, before she says, 'Bitch, I'll burst you fucking worse, you come here again, you understand?'

And then her hand goes to her nose, her finger, finds her nostril, enters, comes back out with a snot about that size, or bigger, says, 'Don't fuck around with the Alpha Nigger...' wipes the snot in my hair '... you hear?' says 'Au revoir' with another punch which crunches the bones in my nose, and stars explode in my head, and this is really boding bad indeed; see the fucking ogre fume and seethe while I sway and bleed and decide that I dearly need to be somewhere not here.

So, I turn with a wobble, hobble toward the gate, get through it. My dinner leaps up into my throat and I spew it, dousing the street, hearing the sound of retreating laughter, a door closing after.

After which I wander again in my stupor, come to a greasy-spoon and enter, head for the ladies room to check my eye which is swelling nicely. Christ, she got me good, I think, as I clean my face of blood at the sink, my hair of snot, use toilet roll to blot it dry, then order tea and take a seat and sip, my will diminished, concede defeat: that's it; I'm finished; beat...

Light up on B.

B

Every night at five...

A

...the odds too tough...

B

...I leave work...

A

...I've had enough.

Light down on A.

B

…and meander the minute or so to McGurk's; sink one, sink two, then bid adieu to the barman – his reply to me each and every time, 'God bless' – depart then, head to the M&S, my dinner to purchase, my day-to-day to adhere to, near to identical all, said days, near rote, you know? Near reflex now.

The bus home then, the silent flat. No cat nor any kind of pet. The sofa – sit. The telly – hit the remote. Reward – the illusion of presence through voices.

Unpack my choices of purchase. Wine: pour, then sip it. My meal: unseal, then flip it into the microwave: shepherd's pie, my favourite dish. Now, why on earth would I think that mattered?

Shattered as shit tonight, I sit, sort through some bills. The telephone trills, my wine spills on my lap. I curse, say, 'Fuck,' pick up.

'Hello?'

'Hello!'

It's Lee, who wants to know if I'd like to go for a drink with herself and Lenny, her loving hubby.

I refuse politely. Lonely as I might be, as I am, I can't abide or suffer the fucker, his swagger, his subtle suggestions; insinuations intimating coupling, couple of times a touch in passing – my behind, my back – Lee's lack of acknowledgement disappointing. But, what's worse is that his vying for me's not just fun. He's overcome when I'm around with a want that's potent and profound, which, bound together with his sleaziness, causes me a great deal of unease, I guess.

My shepherd's pie beeps and I take it, make to unwrap it. The covering jams so I jerk and unjam it with too much force, so it flips and falls – face first, I predict, and am proved correct – the plummet's conclusion a meeting of meat and floor, in effect, aborting my dinner.

I stare at the mess a moment, unmoving, the checking of tears proving fruitless. Doubtless a symptom of self-isolation, the crushing frustration that ushers one night to the next. Tonight more pronounced, the attack unannounced; my reaction surprising me equally. 'Fuck it,' I utter, and phone Lee back, tell her I've changed my mind in fact.

She says, 'Great. How's nine?' An hour. Enough time to shower and so forth, check before I go forth, for keys. Pockets. I can't leave without them. Empty. Now, where the hell did I put them? The kitchen, the counter, swipe them, stop. The slop. I won't bother cleaning it up.

The bus, the seat behind the driver; tactics for the immediate future: forebearance, endurance, tolerate Lenny; have patience when he tries to harass me.

He doesn't, surprisingly. Half an hour there, or here, so far, he's behaving. We're drinking beer, Lee raving on about saving, the fact that she can't, when her rant is cut short by this dude exhuding sex appeal, who steals a look in passing, stops and curses, 'Fuck!' reverses, and, of course, is a friend of Lenny and Lee's.

'Jesus, what are the chances?' he says, and glances at me with a smile to be filed under, 'Most attractive I've seen in a while'.

He asks can he sit and he's let – sure, why wouldn't he be? – and Lenny and Lee make the introductions. Andy's his name and, although I can't claim to be gifted in conversation, we make a connection, I feel, and whatever rubbish I spiel, he understands, or appears to, at one point, clinks my glass with his, says, 'Here's to you,' and I flush and – shush! – between you and me, I'm fairly smitten, admitting the fact to myself when he puts his hand on mine – oh, man! – and, fine, his appeal is amplified by what I've imbibed, but still. The drill for several years has been bed alone, then tears. Each night a trial, you know, a pain. And, to explain why I've lived this way all this while, this fucking denial. Well, it has a lot to do with…

No, screw it. I might get to it after. For now it's chat and laughter until, having hardly had my fill, closing time is proclaimed. And I'm really pained that the night has waned so fast, and last to leave, we stagger out, three quarters cut, no cabs about, and Andy asks if we want to do something wild.

'Like what?'

'Like wait and see,' and he winks, and everyone looks at me and thinks my hesitation's indecision. It's not. It's realisation that the night's not over yet and I'm set to see it through to its end, to rend asunder this fucking curse I've been under.

And so, not wanting to linger, I nod and then smoulder under Andy's reaction; a smile, then an exclamation: 'Awesome!'

We go, see the slo-mo ebb and flow of pub-spill; the mill, the babble, the rabble of wobbling waywards, exiled and aimless, unlike us as, purposeful and double-file, like kids on a dare, we head who the fuck knows where?

Till we do, till having strolled through several streets, we come to a fence on a building site's circumference, in which there's a gap through which we duck and make our way across the muck to a crane – what the fuck?! – which Andy proceeds to climb, followed by Lee and Lenny.

Fine.

There's many would call time-out right now. However, I vowed to follow wherever he led, so, shaking my head to clear it a little, I demonstrate my fettle in dismissing any hint of misgiving and going. One rung after another, adrenaline flowing, I never falter until I'm in the control box and Andy locks me in his embrace, which reddens my face; this and his kiss, his, 'You did it! I fucking knew you could,' my reward.

And now, at his suggestion, we abandon the box, our performance shocking Lenny and Lee, I'd say; our success no less, though, because – hey, presto! – we're out on the arm, defying harm, perching precarious, unprotected, this vantage point that he's selected, revealing, in a sense, the city's sullied magnificence.

His arm comes around me and squeezes tight. I snuggle in, soak up the sight, then, shit! there to my right is Lee on her hands and knees: 'Can I borrow Andy a minute, please?'

'Sure,' I say, and they make their way back, both crawling, to the control box, and, with a gust of wind, the crane rocks, or sways, but I'm unfazed, my gaze unbroken over Dublin, across its horizon, the moment frozen, then fractured, distracted as I am by Lenny, his sudden appearance beside me.

'Howdy,' he says, with a loom and a leer.

'Howdy back,' I respond, and peer beyond him, searching Andy out and finding Lee's on her knees between his legs, head bobbing, robbing him of breath, his gasps, as Lenny clasps my neck and lifts me, pulls my head to his to kiss me.

And it's suddenly plain what tonight has been: a pantomime, the only aim to obtain me for Lenny – the fucking penny has dropped – but the biggest shock is the certainty of my best friend's brazen complicity.

And, hey now. Pull away now. Watch your step.

He advances. Chance is, retreat is pointless. Still. He reaches, I slip his grip, step back and, blind to behind, I trip and topple and, lacking any space to sprawl, I bounce off the edge of the arm and fall and twist and turn and spurn the earth's unstoppable rise by closing my eyes.

Then – surprise! – a feeling of being cocooned or enfolded – hold it! – interruption, postponement of impact; a brief suspension, the moment hijacked; a second ascension; a sense, not seen, of floating, of flight.

And, eyes squeezed tight and confounded as to why I haven't hit the ground yet, I force them open, hoping, I hope not in vain, that I haven't gone insane when I see a face composed of worms entire, one which appears to acquire expression through their movement. See them elongate and thin to form a grin designed to placate, I assume, which job, at any rate, it isn't doing. Then there's the creature's hooves, its wings, its horns, all these things composed of worms as well; its tail, its prick – it's male – their slick, fat, interwoven shapes, like spiderweb or scaffolding, or a machine whose purpose is to power the creature – and me in his arms – up higher, past my betrayers, who gape in wonder at a death deferred by the timely intervention...

Light up on C.

C

Having pulled in...

B

...of, unless I'm mistaken...

C

...before I get out...

B

...a demon.

Light down on B.

C

...I pop a Locket in my mouth, suck, then bite into the shell and – fucking hell! – the spill of honey? I *never* fail to find it yummy.

Putting the packet back in my pocket for later, I manoeuvre my body out of the motor, meander over and, as I enter, am shouldered aside by three wankers as they swagger past, and the last, thinking it's fucking gas, looks back and, like a roguish retard, laughs.

I pay at the counter and enter this community centre doubling as a disco. This copious Cashel congregation of middle-agers, country-livers, sundry lonely lovelorn fuckers looking for partners.

Though I remark there's plenty of younger stuff as well, and it's difficult enough to quell this desire to leer or stare, provoked by the barely legal bodies soaking, arses jolting, nipples poking, evoking so prevailing a craving, I'm quaking.

Control it, you fuck. Hold it in check lest you wreck any chance of a dance in the slow set, reserved as it is for the nervous, the cautious, such as I, the intensely shy.

A girl walks by – that's the one – and sits at a table. My choice. Not as nice as the rest. Much less so, in fact. What she's lacking in lack of weight or in looks, for me is a plus 'cos her type is unfussy by definition.

And so, I position myself nearby and give her the eye and hope it'll be returned, that I won't be spurned with a sneer.

No fear. She's looking my way now, shyly, smiling coyly, the moment highly charged, I must say and just may, when the music slows, step up and propose she join me on the floor.

It does, I do – 'Hello' – and here we are now, holding each other tightly, her heat against me, breasts and belly inflicting upon me a fucking erection, so I imagine, as I always do, a crew of woodlice; loathsome, heinous; crawling from the tip of my penis. And like that, it wanes and wizens until it isn't a problem any more.

Then, four or so songs on, they end the set and we sit and chat. Her topic of conversation: how forsaken one can feel sometimes, how left behind. And I find myself agreeing, seeing I'm in the selfsame boat, you know? The both of us solitary, pathetic and lonely, only not tonight because now she's inviting me back to her abode for tea, which might be code for a bit of gee.

So, up we get, and as we leave, I'm peeved to see those three fucking humps who bumped me on entry, standing sentry by a car, sneering, nearing the point where they'll point and snigger, call her a pig or a cow, which they do as we pass, defining her ass as elephantine, so forth. So mortifying, but, trying hard to keep my anger at bay, I manage to.

And on the way to her house, under shimmering stars, she spontaneously takes my hand in hers.

Then, once indoors, a musty-smelling cottage, old furniture, the lamps low-wattage, I tell her she's beautiful and she smiles, and for a while we just kiss with caution, uncertain. Then, our ease with each other increasing, harder, with hunger, under the low-lit lamp, the smell of damp suffusing. And, without speaking, under no duress, no awkwardness nor stress, we undress.

And the next few hours just fucking rock. So much so that it's two o'clock when I get back to the car park, which is now deserted.

And, as I traverse it, half-sunk in a reverie, I hear, then see those fuckheads from before, doing skids in a car – my fucking own! – and the zone I'm in becomes their destination, accelerating as they are toward me, looking to floor me, no way to evade or avoid in time, to dodge or dive aside, they're flying.

Then they're not, because suddenly they stop no more than an inch from me, and pop the doors, step out with a couple of two-by-fours and accuse me of calling one a prick, which I deny but am quick to qualify by telling the guy that that's what he happens to be, which floors them before my adrenaline soars and I roar, 'Come on, you fucking whores!'

Then, as they begin to move in, I spin and dip and spin again and whip my blade from my trousers, cut a swathe through these losers.

Number one, I split from crown to chin. He screams and, relishing the din, I hew number two across the throat and gloat as he gouts arterial spray and flays and, Jaysus, pirouettes as jets of blood arc round him, like some kind of fountain.

Two down and counting. Where's the third?

He's mounting the rise at the end, then descending out of sight, so I take flight in fright that he might lose me, find the police, see, fuckin' ID me. How would that be? Bad, no doubt. So I run full out and hit the hill, then top it, trip and spill, head over heels and land and stand and scan my surroundings – damn! – depressed at my findings. I guess my slicings were over-balletic. Pathetic. Relying so much on aesthetics, I got distracted. The focus I needed, I lacked it, which led to my failure here, 'cos the motherfucker's disappeared.

I make my way back to the scene of the crime. Two fellas there, one dead, one dying, whose head I go flying over as I drive away – a bump, a spray of gore on the door and the head's a head no more.

And, heading now towards the smoke, the blood on my paws causes me to re-evoke my severe affliction; an overpowering fear of women, all my life, my propensity, when in their company, to flee for fear of getting sick; and at nearly thirty-six years old, my longing to hold or even kiss one. This one thing undone made me so forlorn, and I'd mourn the fact I lacked the flair for something – singing, say – that way I'd find fame, you see, and they wouldn't blame me when I heaved or be peeved at my crippling shyness.

But of course, this idea was bogus, fake, and I'd lie awake at the end of the day and pray, not only to God, but the Devil too, for the power to woo, the means to destroy this weakness. I was hopeless until hope appeared one night in my room, my fright at first sight, suppressed, I confess, by the thing I missed the most; a kiss, though not from a chick, but Old Nick, the host of all the fucks who fall.

He embraced me with solicitude, said, 'There now. No more solitude,' then took out a contract, prepped it, offered me a deal, which I accepted: my eternal soul the price for a voice the world would rejoice or even shed a tear to hear.

So, I signed it, blinded by my bind to the fine print, a misjudgement that's fairly frequent, I've heard since, in dealing with the Dark Prince.

He left, I slept. Next day, I sang, to see if what had been
guaranteed had come to be. And I couldn't believe when I
opened my mouth what came out: a voice refined, resplendent,
defined by transcendent notes which rose, froze, then dipped
and slipped away without trace, replaced by successors, their
even-betters. Unfettered, they soared, agile yet fragile, there,
then gone, notes dead and reborn, so forth, so on.

Then, called upon one night at a party, full of stout, I stood and
cleared my throat and opened my mouth and nothing came out.
And here among all the hubbub of the pub was the rub: the gift
was worthless. My shyness prevented its sharing. I hadn't the
daring to let flow, to show what I could do, to demonstrate my
true, my new worth, my rebirth in song.

So long I'd been waiting. Fucking Satan! Man, I hate the fuck
for confirming what should have been manifest. Obvious.
Evidence of my lack of sense; stupidity and avidity, combining
to dismantle me.

So now you see why I hate the world and primarily women, and
how I can merrily pick up an ugly one these days, and not vomit
or freeze, just as long as I know that her blood will flow. This is
what gives me the courage to woo, you see, to pursue; the fact
that, by the time we're through, she'll have endured my might.

Like with that girl tonight.

As I speared her from the rear and, while being fucked, she
bucked and brayed, I took my blade and stuck it in, then used
my hand to grope about and pull her nethers inside out, and
sucked on another Locket, looked as, in time with her death
throes, her chest rose and fell – for how long, I couldn't tell –
till she was still and honey spilled onto my tongue as I crunched
the sweet, got to my feet, headed for the latrine, keen to clean
myself of the blood and the gore.

Sure, isn't that what a shower is for?

The moon hangs low, its glow suffusing the undersides of clouds
with light. It's like a shroud, the night, and me, you might presume
– or hope – the cocooned within and, hence, the doomed. Well,
dope: you're mistaken; in terms of the Fat Lady singing…

Light up on A.

A

The waitress nudges me…

C

…listen…

A

…shit, I've been dozing…

C

…the bitch hasn't even entered the building.

Light down on C.

A

…she tells me it's closing time, so I get to my feet, put on my coat, and note as I do that she's staring at me.

'Are you okay?'

'I'm fine,' I say.

'There's a line you can call for that kind of abuse, you know.' She hands me a card. I say, 'Oh,' recognising the number on it as mine. At work, I mean. Anyway. Agreeing to phone as soon as I can and thanking her for the advice – 'You're not alone,' she says – I step outside and, Jesus Christ, am forced to hide by diving into a doorway, striving with all my resolve to dissolve into the black, the pitch, as I track the bitch's progress past…

Celine.

…aghast at the nasty plans she makes regarding Helen with her
mates, two of the ugliest women I've ever beheld, though, in
contrast to their well-fed crony, bodywise, they're pretty bony,
skinny, and both of them give a whinny at Celine's design to
find her pregnant 'concubine' – her word, not mine – and get rid
of the kid to come with a broom, its handle pruned to a taper
with which they'll rape her and puncture in the process, the
unborn fucking fetus.

'Jesus,' I think, or maybe say, as I see that the peril she's in is
worse than hitherto presumed. And, assuming this gruesome
deed goes ahead, she's doomed, at the very least, to be ruined,
or worse, to be dead.

That being said, I'd be pretty deranged to endanger myself a
second time, so why am I spying on the sluts, following as they
strut about, flouting the details of their mission to one and all by
acting it out? Their appalling impressions of Helen, compelling
in a macabre way. It's as if how they cry and beg and plead is
borne of a need to see this scene made real. They can't conceal
their glee, their excitement.

As for me, I keep my distance, using trees for cover, doorways,
other things.

Celine picks up a rock and flings it into the air, and it lands on a
car, and she whistles a carefree tune out loud, the aim the
appearance of blamelessness.

And look how fucking proud she is.

See her knock an old woman aside outside a shop. See the
woman fall and wish I could stop, but not wanting to lose my
prey, I leap her arm, outflung, and continue on my way.

And, further along, a gang, four-strong, of intimidating blokes,
hang out, intimidating passing folks till seeing Celine and co.
draw near, they clear a path, as if in fear, by separating.

I go round, of course, capitulating to *them*, when – damn! – I
feel a flurry of fright as my quarry disappears from sight into

Pearse Street Station, necessitating my rushing across the road and dashing inside and pushing through the crowd to the idling train, having already spied the bitches boarding seconds before.

I squeeze through the doors as they close, then, like some private detective, I suppose, I'm pretty effective in keeping my cover, pretty selective as to my seat, fleet of foot enough in getting my butt to one at the other end and blending in unseen as three packets of Sour Cream & Onion Pringles are produced by the odious pack, a snack for the trip, a little treat, which they pop open then and eat with uncanny concentration as the train careers from station to station.

And after a certain length of time, some associations occur in my mind. I'm comparing Helen and her mother, you see, their falling out, to my daughter and me, our own separation, brought about by…

That's a glaring omission.

Shit.

That's right. I've a child of my own. 'A child!' She's more than fully grown. And the oversight can perhaps be explained by the fact that she and I've been estranged for several years, and that talking about her often induces tears in me, so I tend to refrain. Bear with me, though, and entertain any crying I might do, and I'll try my best to explain exactly how, around the time of her father's death, her body, like that, just seemed, I don't know, to blossom and bloom. My bone of contention, the seed of my ruin, all the attention it was accruing, while mine, still attractive, became neglected.

So, the fellas she brought home, I'd flirt with. 'Hi,' I'd say, my hips asway, and utter something like, 'He's cute' – see the fella blush – or 'a beaut', or admire the fella's tush, or rush into the room when they were all alone in my nightie: 'Where the hell's my phone?' That kind of flighty flirty stuff, not bad enough to be consequential.

That is, until the arrival of Ray, who was far from unaffected by my suggestive eye, who on the day of the night she said that he was the one she'd wed, I took him to bed.

Led by what?

Well, my excuse was that we were just too close in age – I'd
had her too young – but sageness borne of remorse has taught
me that, of course, the fault was all my own, my behaviour
begotten by the rot in my soul that told me it wasn't fit that she
should go with while I went without; envy no doubt, inciting
me to destroy the thing that frightened me: her contentment.

And my resentment so strong, I contrived that my trysts with
Ray would go on long after, her none the wiser, and then, to
prise her from him for ever, I left a letter in a book I knew she'd
look at, one he wrote to me, in which, for her to see, was
evidence of incidents and rendezvous and 'I love you's.

But, in my ruse, I was too short-sighted to see that, slighted, she'd
take her grudge and never budge in its execution; my renunciation
her objective, carried out with such invective, effective even after
her suicide endeavour, a failure, as were my many attempts to see
her, which I quit in time, and, shit, some nights I wake up crying,
knowing it's her I've been dreaming about.

Some days I doubt I can live my life another minute without her
in it.

Anyway.

I didn't cry.

We stop and a girl hops on and flops across from our friends
and removes her hat and, just like that, she's peppered with
Pringles, a shower, most of which adhere securely to her curly
hair, and sure, she could pick them out of there, but in front of
the harpies, she doesn't dare. What she does instead is just sit
and stare ahead, abiding patiently, till, arriving at the next
station she can get up and go. But, as she does, she's grabbed
and, in no uncertain terms, is told to 'Sit the fuck back down,'
and, scared as she is, she obeys, of course, held by their gaze,
the force of their glare, as they begin to pluck the Pringles from
her hair, the bitches, and eat them, saying, 'Mm, Delicious!'
after every munch, the crunch only coming when they've eaten
them all and the girl has the gall to ask, 'Can I go now?'

And, oh, how I know to my own regret, what kind of response that's gonna get.

Now, watch as Celine leans forward, grabs her by the throat and squeezes, causing the girl to wheeze and say, 'Please!' as the grip is tightened, everyone frightened, looking away, and Celine says, 'Say, "My hair is muck",' and she does, through tears.

Now, look, as Celine rears back, then attacks her with her head – a butt – which comes away red, having cut up the poor girl's face, and, again spraying spit, she says, 'That's what you get for thinking you're fucking it!' then pulls her up by the curls, hauls her to the door and hurls her out – we're stopped, by the way – then shouts, 'Oh, hey!' and follows her off and returns, a single Pringle held aloft, and says, 'One left! Ha-ha!' and eats it and beats it back to her seat as the train moves on again, her skinny buddies overcome with a fit of whinnies – 'Oh, shit,' says one, 'I'm gonna piss in me fucking ninnies!'

...which only end as they're descending a few stops on, me tagging along in a kind of stalk over the walkover, down and past the ticket-seller, up one street and then another, into the doorway of a shop, in which, as one, the bitches drop their pants and push and hot steam rises with a whoosh! as piss cascades in a gushing blast for what seems like ages, till, at last, Celine says 'Jesus,' as the streams decrease, then cease, 'Fucking relief!' and then they're off again, coming to a pub a couple of streets away and going in.

And now my nerves begin to jump, my heart to pump, the both of which I try to still by steeling my will, and just stepping inside and stepping aside into a sort of snug, unseen, and gleaning what's going on by peeking around the partition, my position affording me a view of the few in the room; Celine, of course, her team, and, not for the first time tonight, an ex-pupil of mine: Joe White, behind the bar. At the time, by far the most unpleasant child in school.

He was wild, unruly, truly reviled, and, weird, the only person he feared was his mother. Who the hell knows why? I'd seen her make him cry with no more than a disapproving look, then make him happy again with no more than an unexpected grin.

He brings the bitches a bottle of gin, returns behind the bar and, so far, no Helen. Then, as they're telling him about their exploits on the train, she enters from the ladies, looking like Hades heated, defeated, stressed, her body best described as slight, despite the enormous bump which proceeds her as she heeds her tormentor's call to come and sit at the table, unable to look at Celine as she proclaims her love in tender tones, the cronies cooing, but also makes no bones about what needs doing tonight, and will be done, as soon as Helen downs the bottle of gin.

'Now, begin,' she says.

And, without a word of protest to this grotesque, Helen lifts the bottle to her lips and sips, then steadily gulps, her swallowing loud, a proud Celine encouraging her a bit: 'Keep going, love,' she says. 'That's it…'

Then, shit! I hit against a chair.

Then, fuck! The atmosphere goes cold as I hold my breath and huddle, befuddled by the lull that's descended, the silence, rendered frozen by the sudden threat of violence.

Did they hear me? Are they near me now?

After an interlude, I conclude that they didn't. They're not. Then, hearing 'Caught you, you cunt!' know I'm sorely mistaken and, shaking in fear, I look up and she's there, a fucking chair above her head, its port of call, my own.

Then there's the fall, my moan, the downward arc, the crack, the dark into which I sink, the blackness, thinking with an inward smile…

Light up on B.

B

We fly through town…

A

…'It's not so bad here…'

B

…all over…

A

'…maybe I'll stay a while.'

Light down on A.

B

…one end to the other and back, and the fact that I feel like I've lost my mind doesn't blind me to the thought that the demon's showing off or playing a game; right now we're keeping pace with a train; now gaining speed, now leading it, leaving it behind, winding our way back through the city, flying lower now; it's pretty scary, the many hairy turns we take – for Jaysus' sake! – we nearly clip a steeple, people unaware below, missing the show, feeling the after-blow and supposing it's just a breeze as our passing shakes the trees, dislodges leaves, and we're gone, continuing on post-haste, though with no little grace, to the coast where, at last, we descend to Dollymount, the beach, and land, and the demon beseeches me sit in the sand, then asks me my name and I tell him and then for a spell, we're quiet. Can't say I enjoy it, looking out to sea, not really having a clue what to say.

But then I do, and, screwing my courage to the sticking place and, prefacing my question with, 'No offence…'

'None taken,' he says.

…I ask what he is.

A pause, then he laughs a little drolly. 'I'm a soul,' he says, 'but the body I lived in isn't dead. I was sold to Satan for the going rate and I'm here to reclaim my erstwhile "host", I suppose he's called.'

Here he stalls as a worm crawls away from his face and falls to the sand and hastens away, and he chases it, grabs and replaces it just above his chin. 'There's always one,' he says, and continues on, telling me that he'd gone and escaped from Hell, his dwelling quarter, 'Sort of recruited this suit to give me form,' he says.

'Why worms?' I ask

'Because they're the norm for those who return, and have been for infinity. Their proximity to the dead, you see, engenders an affinity. Hence what you see.'

'I see,' I say. 'And, what did he sell you for? If you don't mind me asking.'

And he tells the tale of a virgin verging on giving up the ghost, who, like Faust, was offered a pact which lacked a certain clause, which caused him to be deceived and not to receive what he believed he would; that is, to become, through song, some kind of stud: 'Who, when I find him,' he goes on, 'will know a reprimanding way beyond his mortal comprehending.'

'Really?'

'Fuckin' A. Motherfucker has to pay, man.' Then he gives me a look like he's racking his brain, says, 'What the fuck were you doing up on a crane?' the explaining of which is a bitch, but I give him it all, from phone call to fall, and he listens rapt, only interrupting to react to certain nefarious points in my tale with various comments like, 'That's a bit vile!' or, 'I like your style,' or, 'Oh, man, I can taste the fucking bile in my mouth!' when I come to the bit about the betrayal. 'I mean, she was your mate!' meaning Lee, and I agree and he says, 'See? We both got fucking betrayed!'

It's strange, but there's a desire in there to please I think, or impress. Unless I'm misreading the creature, his nature, the shyness behind his bluster which allows me to muster up the courage to ask him what it is he wants with me.

But he doesn't respond. He's watching the sea again and, as I follow his eye, I spy in the distance, creatures a little like him in appearance, closing fast, and I gasp as he clasps me again in his arms and beats his wings and above the explosion of sand they create, we ascend, take flight and expedite ourselves in the other direction.

But, fast as we hasten, they're closing the gap; he's becoming handicapped by his freight, my weight. We keep going, straight across the city centre, then the suburbs, subsequently the country, our mile head start curtailed to half a mile, soon after a quarter. And now, a little further, we falter, fall toward a wood and filter through the trees, and when we should hit ground, we don't at all, it's through we fall, into a small place, a crack in the earth, a crawlspace, and crawl is what the demon does, propelling us, face frowning, ever down. I look behind and find we've been joined by our hunters, shunting into the bind, the breach, each set of eyes, ever bright, never waning, ever gaining, no abstaining in pursuit relentless. My demon senses their closeness and I almost give up the ghost as a worm hand brushes my heel, but then I feel a stealing away of solid, an expanding of space, and again we plummet, no obstacle now to wings unfurling, hurling us faster in our descent, their hell-bent beating thrusting us through the tunnel, then dropping us into a cavern, whose colossal proportions we cross, performing en route a fucking loop-the-loop, before shooting for a crack in the facing wall, the gap too small, it seems, to suffice, but our entry's precise, exact, meticulous, an inch on either side of us, then widening once we're in, and again we're in tunnel transit, racing, tracing its twisting, turning route, glimpsing offshoots, other tunnels, shooting past, their value moot to us, until it's not. Until we brake, decelerate, and, into one we slip and stop and linger just inside the lip, unseen, as our pursuers seem in effect to reflect their ferocity in velocity as they blast past so fucking fast I'm cast back by the wind of their wingbeat, almost off my feet, in fact, and, as their sound retreats, then

fades away, I sigh, turn to the demon, say: 'Well, hey.' He
contemplates me, curiously; then, his worm-mouth stretching
tight, he smiles, says, ' "Hey" is right.'

A short while later, we situate ourselves by a river, a silver
sliver slithering through this dark delirium, where I query him
as to who our pursuers were. For a moment he stares, then says,
'You don't want to know.'

But I do. 'Were they souls like you?'

'Uh-huh.'

'From Hell? Come to quell your little rebellion?'

'No,' he says. 'They're from Heaven, and they're the ones
given the task of setting wrong things right.'

'Like what?' I ask.

'Like you tonight,' he says, 'not dying in your fall.'

I pale at this, appalled, and fail to stall a stricken cry, then say,
'So, what? Am I going to die?'

The worms contort as he nods to fashion his face into one of
compassion then, and as my world comes crashing in, he takes
my hand and gives me a look so understanding that it doesn't
seem ugly in any way to let him hug me, and there I stay,
remembering, for some reason or other, the fight I had that night
with my mother.

The tone she took when, in a book, marking her page, sparking
my rage, I discovered a note in which was written that a certain
man was smitten, infatuated, and glad the feeling was
reciprocated. And, of course, the letter's author was the would-
be fiancé of the lover's daughter. Me. And so we fought, or
rather, I raged and ripped the page and mocked her age and
cried and swore I'd die before I spoke to her again. Then, bereft
of both, I left, the rift to persist up to and past their split, which
fact, gave me cause for bitter delight, short-lived, I'll admit,
because, tonight, I wish with death so near that she was here to
wipe a tear or stroke my hair or say, 'There, there.'

But she's not and I've got to settle instead for my demon, in whose embrace I abide till my tears subside and, having pulled myself together a bit, I say, 'Shit!'

'What's that?'

'I left the shower on last night.'

He nods. 'Oh right,' and I let out a bitter titter, realising how little it matters as one of the fatter worms escapes from his ear, which, this time, *I* ensnare and restore before it occurs to me to ask why at all he bothered in saving me from my fall if my death was preordained.

And suddenly, he looks ashamed.

'I had no choice,' he explains. 'Whatever the price, I had to touch a woman. So long, you see, without form; so long forlorn and mourning the fact that I never had, and sad that I never would, I knew with my body of worms, their flesh and blood, that I could. So, chancing to spot you mid-plummet I caught you. I'm sorry if I upset you, but just, you know, to have met you, I...'

There's a gap as he stares at his lap and squirms and a hundred thousand worms turn red in a blush and he raises his head as I take his hand and, for reasons I don't really understand – my impending death, maybe, or gratitude, or sympathy – I become imbued with a want that won't be suppressed.

And, at my behest, he puts his hand on my breast, and, not really knowing what else to say, I just smile and tell him, 'Touch away.'

Then I'm nude, no prudishness, just bliss as we kiss and caress and he presses me down, no sound but our breathing. I find myself needing to take him inside me and say so, and, spreading me wide, he says, 'Guide me,' and in he goes and we're soon in the throes of passion, both of us thrashing about, shouting with pleasure, its measure beyond the counting, yet ever mounting, his love-making also entailing trailing his tail about my body, between my thighs, eliciting cries, over my belly and, fuck, I'm

jelly beneath his administrations, his tail's manipulations, his
hunger. I don't think I can hold out any longer. He's killing me,
causing me to convulse and spasm…

Light up on C.

C

I spot a guy…

B

…as we peak, then tip into the chasm…

C

…beside a ditch…

B

…so to speak, of mutual orgasm.

Light down on B.

C

…he's trying to hitch a ride, and, like that, I decide to brake and
make a Samaritan gesture: 'Come on over, enter, rest your
weary feet. You must be beat.'

'I am,' he replies and slides in beside me, wise in taking my
offer up, in luck. Or maybe not. A lot depends for him on whim,
my own. Knife honed and keen, whatever way I lean come
time, could dictate his living or dying.

He's a quiet type, doesn't make a peep, but given the hour and
falling asleep, so I ask him his name, which is Shane, and
explain the situation, my need for conversation.

He begins a tale, then, after a hesitation, that doesn't fail to keep
my attention; pretty moving; pretty wrenching; filled with
deeply felt emotion. And throughout the entire account, he
cries, and I'd be telling lies if I said I didn't empathise.

He'd been seeing a girl for a year and it's clear he adored her, so
much so, he ignored her bored 'I suppose' when he came to
propose, and thought, That's okay. It's her way. Till the day
when he called and was simply appalled to be told by her father
she'd said that she'd rather be dead than be wed to such a joke,
so instead had fled to the smoke where some bloke she'd seen
in the past had called from and asked her to come and stay for a
day or two. And so, to eschew any blame or the need to explain,
she had taken the train. And, when he asked her father why
she'd changed her mind, his eyes half-blind behind the tears
which lined his face, the father braced himself and said, 'Look.
I know this is tough, but, fuck… you just weren't good-looking
enough.' And so – yeah, I know – in the days that followed, he
wallowed about in despair, then became aware of a yen in his
heart to see her once again, her face, before starting his life
anew, alone, as best he could with his future blown. And that's
where he was going when I picked him up.

He tucks himself against the door, stops sobbing, snores. I
watch him doze, understanding, I suppose. He farts, poor
fucker. And again. This one deeper. A seeper. But how can I
take offence? An odour relents, but the intensity of a loss like
his is a cross that endures. And I wonder if yours truly's not the
lucky one never to have loved at all than loved and lost if that's
the cost.

I turn the radio on, move the dial till I find a song, moodwise
wrong for this time of night; too light, but not the worst. What
follows, though, is choice, a burst of Bette, whose voice I let
wash over me as she sings, 'The Wind Beneath My Wings'.
Though it stings a bit to admit that I could do that shit much

better without even breaking sweat, and yet, no one will ever
know. It boils my fucking blood. Though Bette's rendition, still
very good, is enough to cool it again.

At least till it ends and the news comes on and I learn that the
guy I failed to eliminate went straight to the station, gave the
police my vehicle's make and registration and a good description
of my face, which they reiterate and state that, 'If you see this
guy, just walk away, don't try to apprehend him. He…'

Ah, man, this shit's offending me, so I change the station,
attempting to control my temper, when I hear a whimper and
look over, see Shane cower, quake in terror. I make a gesture,
stutter, 'Hey, man. That's not me.' His answer: a wee. You can
see the spreading blotch across his crotch, the smell of which is
rich with dread and fear, so I say, 'Is what I said not clear? It's
someone else they're talking about!' But, no. The stupid fuck
lets out a shout and grabs my throat and squeezes and squeals.

Then, that's all she wrote because, Jesus, the wheels just turn of
their own volition; we're out of control and then there's a
collision. A pole. And, one second he's there, the next: thin air.
He wasn't wearing his seatbelt, see, and so was catapulted
through the windscreen. This has-been or once-was, so-called
because he's no more. Though just to make sure, I open the door,
step out, spit glass from my mouth, get walking and find him.
Still alive, but only just, he's busted up and in serious pain. So I
squat and explain I can end it fast with an elegant little *coup de
grâce*, but he'd rather not, and I've got to respect his decision.

'In that case, I've something will lessen rather than hasten the
pain of your passing.' I reach into my pocket, produce my pack
of Lockets, hand them to him, telling him not to chew them,
rather, suck. He looks at me like I'm thick. 'That way they
won't be gone as quick.' But the prick doesn't heed me,
unwraps them speedily, munches them greedily, displeases me
with his gluttony. I shouldn't be so touchy, though. As such, he
deserves to eat however he feels, it being his final meal. So, this
in mind, I sit beside him, hold his hand, say, 'Munch away, my
friend. I understand.' And off he goes and on his last one, his

chewing slows and before he's done, he dies with a sad but pretty sated grin, some honey running down his chin.

Now, I don't intend to be mean or give that impression, but he could've left me one in the spirit of absolution.

Fuck it. Benediction said, I turn on my heels and head across fields, having decided to avoid the road for now. And, somehow, 'neath the moon so bright and bold, reflecting again on the tale my buddy told tonight, my own plight doesn't seem as heavy. So, at a steady pace and with a couple of upbeat songs, which now I whistle, now I hum, I continue on.

Though it isn't long before my good cheer disappears, and hunger and fears of being lost accost me. Field to field, my travels fail to yield any sign of civilisation, just this proliferation of green, these gates to climb, this uneven terrain to traverse, this merciless cold, this fatigue, this league of griefs, this stream which I leap and see how deep it is when my jump falls short and my foot goes in – up to my shin.

Or continuing on at a clip and tripping, falling into shit – my hand – and standing, spotting a cow right there who watches with an air of ridicule – 'You fool!' – of contempt which causes me to vent my spleen by wiping clean my hand of stink on his flanks, his face, his neck: 'Who's laughing now, you bovine fuck?'

As I walk, I'm scoping all the time, hoping for a sign of something living – cows don't count. Or sheep – It's people I'm looking for, a car – how far have I come so far on foot, each grievous step proving harder than the previous? Far enough I've almost given up, when, coming over a hill, I see a filling station down below and, filled with elation, down I go, discovering as I do, there's an all-night shop attached whose hatch I reach, whose resident I beseech – these fellas are always murder – 'Get the fuck up and take my order!'

And just to abuse him a bit for his sullen demeanour, I begin, much to his chagrin – all the trips he has to make – to order a rake of fucking things: a packet of onion rings, a Turkish Delight, two cans of Sprite, a Flyte, a Twirl, a Curly Wurly, a

packet of Buffalo Hunky Dorys, a Sherbert Dip, a coffee, a
Walnut Whip, a Toffee Crisp, a Wispa, please, some Chickatees,
some bacon fries – this stage, the guy's in a rage as he flies back
and forth – a Lucozade Sport, an Aero, a Moro, a packet of
Rolo, a packet of Polo, a packet of Monster Munch, a Brunch, a
couple of Crunchies... I've a hunch he's gonna blow, so, last
but not least – hope they have it in stock, it's... yes! – a packet
of Lockets.

I sit outside and start to eat, and woe betide my heart, the way
I'm treating it. Then, completing it, my little feast, I'm spent, so
I relent to sleep's release, however short, interrupted by the
arrival into the forecourt of a truck, some clown who jumps on
down, his keys left in the ignition, positions himself at the hatch
and orders twenty blue, which is my cue to do what needs doing
and, rueing the fact I lack the knack to drive a truck like this, I
reckon I'll get the gist. So, I up and meander toward it, climb on
board it, find the accelerator, floor it, see the clown turn round –
'What the fuck?!' – with such a look of surprise that laughter
rises to my throat and I gloat as he follows at a run, dumbstruck,
the dumb fuck, I think, and no mistake, as I leave the wanker in
my wake.

So, here we are now, back on the road. I'm loaded full of chow,
my coffee's culled my need for sleep for now. As long as I can
keep at liberty till Dublin, then I'll see if I can't dump the rig
somewhere and disappear into that big concealing town. So,
vowing to arrive before dawn, I suppress a yawn and increase
my speed, paying no heed to the limit, succeeding in keeping
the pace all the way to Portlaoise where, shit, the leash of the
law is produced at last, or the noose, represented by the
appearance and pursuit of several Garda cars.

And it occurs to me that she's probably in the building now, the
lady I spoke about, who's overweight, whose singing indicates
the culmination of the show, its end, and though I understand
that this means *mine*, I swear I'm not gonna get caught for want
of trying. So, putting the pedal to the floor while unwrapping
another Locket, and whoring ahead like a rocket, I concentrate
on outrunning my fate, frustrated...

Light up on A.

A

A few years younger…

C

…never having suspected…

A

…in bed with my daughter…

C

…It would arrive so unexpectedly.

Light down on C.

A

…a bottle of red and assorted treats on a tray – a selection of cheeses, fresh cream and peaches – a girls' night in with each of us drying the other's eyes when the other cries at the film unfolding on screen.

This is not a dream, but a memory. One of my dearest, the merest detail of which hasn't waned at all. Except one: what the hell the movie was called.

And as I strain to recollect, a pain, the effect of having been decked by a chair, interferes and conspires to wake me and make me face my plight, which now I do and face the sight of Joe White, standing over me, posed with prick in hand, eyes closed and jacking off, as they say, to beat the band.

And, hey! My breasts are exposed, my legs are splayed, I'm posed as a visual aid to his self-delight, the dirty shite.

He hears me move and jumps in fright and tries to put his thing away, to explain, as I rise, ignoring the pain behind my eyes, look into his, say, 'Joe?' And he says, 'Miss?' the fool, like we're still in school back when.

'Where are they, gone?' I ask. He doesn't know, or so he says, and so I quiz him, recalling his Achilles heel, as to how he'd feel if I asked his mother instead.

Silence, then success as his face goes red, and he confesses that they headed down to the cellar seconds before, then implores me not to tell.

'Please, Miss!'

Ignoring this, I squeeze behind the bar, hoping to find some kind of weapon there and do, a hurley stick, then, stepping out, I tell the prick I'll keep my mouth shut if he leaves, which, thanking me repeatedly as he goes – 'You're tough but fair, Miss,' he says – he does.

And I fairly buzz with anticipation as I go to the door in the floor, blood racing, amazed at the sudden replacing of fear with determination, my spur no longer Helen, rather an overwhelming desire to chasten Celine, to break her down, to punish and purge her for what she's done. To hurt her. This is the urge I'm overcome with, here at the point of no return.

Which point I pass right there and then in opening the door, descending in a crouch, seeing Helen, naked on a couch, too drunk to fight as the cronies pull her legs apart and Celine moves in between them, sharpened stick at the ready, saying, 'Hold her steady, bitches!' which is as much as she gets out before her mouth is shut by a smack from my stick, and the shock on her face as she turns is erased by my second blow, much worse than the first, which bursts her lip and rips a rupture in her face.

Her response is she launches a counter-attack of punches – seven, or even eight, my hunch is – the last of which is the one that pitches me onto my back, then the bitch's hands are around my neck and she croons as asphyxiation looms, 'Nigger, give up; you're doomed; you're dead.'

But I don't. Instead, my hands whip out and grip her face like a vice and my thumbs find their way to her eyes and I dig them in and they begin to collapse into her skull as she tries to pull away and cries and prays and pleads for me to stop, to no avail.

And then a 'Pop!' as my fingernail penetrates and the eye deflates and fluid drains and a second later, the second does the same and, half-unhinged, I lunge for the stick I dropped and pick it up and bring it down on her face as many times as it takes for my blood to cool a little and, drooling spittle, I turn to the other pair, standing there in a trance, nearly shitting their pants, and advance, and they turn and bolt up the stairs like a couple of colts, maybe, or mares, only really skinny, and minus now any trace of fucking whinny.

Helen's out cold, but seems to be fine. I sit and hold her hand in mine and, overcome by what I've done, start crying, then succumb to sleep. A dumb mistake, because when I wake at last, I see that hours have passed, so I give her a shake, no time to lose, she opens her eyes, half-blind with the booze. And, as I could have guessed, she can't even stand, so I get her dressed and manhandle her up the stairs, bearing her weight, through the bar, to the street, my muscles giving me hassle as I hustle her in haste and try to trace whatever route is right to bring about a flight from here to somewhere more secure.

And, right there, we procure a taxi, get into the back seat, journey mutely under passing lights, the night at an end, day pending, or rather morning.

And as I watch its approaching glow, a massive melancholy grows as questions are posed, like: should or could I have stopped her any other way than to slay her? I ponder and, to my dismay, discover there was a simpler option. I could have just walked away. Forgotten. But I'm a killer now. I've crossed the line, and, though my crime weighs heavy upon me, I consider this girl beside me and ask myself would I do it again and decide I would. I believe the bad I did engendered good, that the life of Celine for Helen's child, in the scheme of things was a fitting trade.

And, before this thought can fade, she speaks, asks why I did what I did.

'To save your kid.'

'But I wanted it dead.'

'You what?' She shakes her head and a knot in my stomach appears, as do tears in her eyes as she tries to articulate, in her still sodden state, what the child will have to endure through the cataclysmic disorder which, it's been discovered, afflicts it, no way to fix the damage to its brain, the perpetual pain of a body whose bones over time will contort and mutate and distort and deteriorate, 'Its fate a living hell,' she says, and she touches the swell of her belly and maybe the crying's catching, 'cos now I'm matching her tear for tear as she says, 'I can't bear to let her live. I can't.'

And I want to dispute the point, to persuade her to relent, to scold her and chide her. Instead I just hold her, seeing only the woe that's about to betide her; her love for what's inside her the only motive for its murder; one of genuine compassion, as ill-designed and imperfectly schemed as it had been.

A moment later, we're jerked a bit, the car having braked so as not to hit a guy on a bike, and, what's new? the driver starts to spew invective, ineffective, but in light of our need for peace, no less a pest, so I request that he stop – politely, lest he blow his top, as tightly wound as these guys can be – as they are, because this one stops the car and turns, his face gone pink, and says, 'You think you can talk to me how you want?'

He then comes round from the front...

'In my car, you cunt?'

... and opens the door and grabs me out...

'You can't!'

...then Helen, both of us spilling onto Ormond Quay, then he gets back in and drives away and I begin to say, 'The fuck!' when a truck comes down the Quay, a fleet of police cars in pursuit. And, the truth is, I'm mesmerised by its size, I suppose, its velocity, frozen possibly by its imposing nature, its thunder and weight, sure, approaching like fate, sure.

And, a second too late, I reach out and say, 'Stop!' and Helen steps into the road, in front of the truck, and sort of implodes as she's sucked beneath, then dragged a bit, about twenty feet, then released, and, shit, the least he could do is stop, but he doesn't, though the cop cars do.

Then, the men in blue are running about, one squatting down to check her out and finding that, despite her bleeding, she's breathing.

Shit. A crowd appears. I sit. An ambulance veers to a stop.

I smoke a cigarette, then midway through it, happen to notice I'm being spoken to. A bloke, asking exactly who I was to the deceased. And, right then, Christ, I comprehend she's gone and, even though I'm not, respond, 'Her mom.' And the guy whistles long and loud, calls, 'John!' and a man appears from the crowd, which cheers, and proudly but gently hands me a bloodstained baby, bundled up, a beauty, which I watch, completely captivated.

And, somehow, after this ill-fated night, my failed crusade, misguided right from the start, this child does something to my heart, recalls to me my own child's birth, the sense I had of being earthed to the world as joy unfurled around me, bound me to her and, through her, made me whole. And my soul is suddenly filled with the need to see her face, just once, to embrace, to erase for a moment, all trace of this with a kiss, to say, 'I miss you,' even if in vain, to explain, to ascertain the name of the film we watched in bed that time with our wine and our treats, to express regret, to set myself at her feet and accept whatever judgement she sees fit to exact. And I'm panicked by how little time I've left before I'm remanded and payment's demanded for my theft of life.

The guy takes the baby away, but not before I put my lips to its ear and say…

Sure, fuck it; what does my pointless patter matter, anyway? A kiss goodbye and they disappear into the crowd, the attention they inspire allowing me to quietly retire.

I drift down one street, then a second, trekking towards a taxi rank, which I pass this time – no thanks – and choose the bus instead and get on and we head – no hurry; I'm betting, this early, she's only getting out of bed.

And, then I'm there, and, Christ, no fear heretofore can compare with what I'm feeling now. Though, somehow I quell it and ring her bell. It doesn't bring a response, so I chance a couple of knocks. No luck, so I look in the letterbox, see through to the kitchen, in which, on the floor, is a microwave meal, its wrapper half-peeled, then revealed, not to my eyes, but my ears, is the noise of a running shower.

She's here.

And at this early hour, though way too late, I wait, contemplating my life, my fate, my regret for all the things I've done and endured, the distance I've come, my darling girl…

Light up on B.

B

Lying there…

A

…to end up here…

B

…like a bride…

A

…outside your door.

Light down on A.

B

…my head on his chest, I hide as best I can from thoughts of what's to come. After a while, I look up with a smile, which he doesn't see, engulfed as he seems to be in introspection.

'What is it?' I ask him.

'Nothing.'

'Tell.'

'I think I'm in love with you.'

'Well,' I say, 'That's typical of a guy; to fall for the very first girl you fuck.'

'Have sex with,' he corrects with, suddenly coy.

'Make love to,' I say, enjoying our ease with each other, our simple rapport which, unfortunately, is smothered when I kiss him and tell him I'll miss him and this impulsive confession succeeds in quashing our passion and pushing us into a woebegotten mood in which each of us broods on the looming termination of our barely blooming relationship.

'Maybe I'll see you in Hell,' I say, and he smiles in a way that breaks my heart, then says, 'Come here,' and now we start to make love again, the act a form of medicine to jettison all thought of what we're caught within; our movements rendered slow and tender by regret at being star-crossed lovers badly met.

And now, as we come to the end, with a gust of wind, they descend, the seven angels who portend my death. And, yes. I get the lack of similarity now, the disparity, how their wings are feathery, not leathery in look, the fucking beauty of their forms, spectacular despite the fact that they're also made of worms.

The leader speaks, says to my demon, 'If you think you can hinder fate, you're dreaming. Now disappear so we can do our duty here.'

He hesitates a bit, as if somehow irresolute, then kisses me on the mouth; a kiss goodbye I presume, then doubt, when I see his eyes assume a determination which burns as he turns to the angels and tells them, 'No…'

They just look.

'…I won't let her go,' and he swells his chest and closes his fists and insists, 'The first one to touch her, believe me, I'll butcher,' the moment fleeting before, with a beating of wings, he flings himself high and waits and the leader sighs and turns to his mates and says, 'Guys?' and all seven ascend and surround my friend…

My what?! No, more than that. A lot. My heart. My short-lived love who prolonged my life so that I might, at the end, understand a love that goes beyond any I've ever known before; a love that, though doomed, is truly pure, personified by the furious fight now raging overhead, a dreadful mass of colliding, crashing, enmeshing, smashing limbs.

My God, the din's intense and, hence, I cover my ears as my demon veers from left to right, punching and biting and fighting with all he's got, every strike that connects detaching a batch of worms which pitch to the ground like a rain all around me.

But his supremacy's fleeting; one second he's beating them hard, the next he's on guard as the sheer amount of them starts to count for them; they no longer the blow-receivers, but the givers, each one sending shivers up my spine as more worms, *his* this time, come raining down on my head, the dreadful sight revealed of his body; flayed, unmade; pieces gone; his shoulder, his chest, so on.

He's thrown against a wall and I call as he falls with a crash and I dash toward him, reach him, and as I hold him, beseech him forget about me, that, my destiny being sealed, he can't be my shield. 'Are you mad?!' 'And have you,' I add, 'forgotten your mission?'

'What?'

'The guy who sold you to Satan. Go and locate him. Do what you said you would. I'm dead.'

He shakes his head, says, 'No.'

'I am,' I insist. 'Go and finish your quest. There's nothing you can do about this!'

He's pissed, but I've gotten through. He touches my face, says, 'I'll miss you too,' then a kiss adieu, a last embrace, held really long, and, like that, he's gone, soaring up from the floor to the ceiling, a final backward look revealing his tears, before he disappears through a crack in the rock, and I'm alone.

And now in a tone without mercy, the leader asks me if I'm ready, to which I reply, 'I don't want to die,' and he sighs as if he sympathises and tells me I should know better, that I don't have any choice in the matter. Then, stepping closer, he whispers in my ear, 'Don't fret, my dear, or fear. It's a piece of cake from here.'

Then he takes my hand and steers me toward the river, and, stepping in, I comprehend with a shiver that this is how it's going to end. And, why, I don't understand, but I smile, somehow reconciled to my fate; no denial, no fight, no fear or attempt at flight; merely descent as the height of the water increases slowly until we're below the surface, the only feeling now, the filling of my lungs; the only sound, the pounding of my pulse; the only sight, a dullish light which abates as my senses relent to my body's intent: to yield to death. Which, at last, it does.

And, here within its fist, in the midst of whatever terminus this is – a void as black as pitch, in which I now exist, it seems, as thought alone, or a dream – I'm shown a stream of memories which, having appeared, immediately cease to be for ever.

Gone. Like severing my wrists on losing Ray. That's wiped
away. Or my very first kiss. That too. The first time I got
pissed, and a slew of others, like feeding at my mother's breast,
wearing pigtails at her behest, the day that I stopped believing
in God – I was ten – the day I started believing again – the
birth of my sister, dead an hour and forty minutes after, my
father's tears of rage, my uncle's leers when I came of age, the
page of my diary I tore out and set on fire, the avowal it held
annihilated, a guy I hated, a poem I created, a tone that grated
and made me shudder, my mother's, when in front of others
she scolded me – these memories, one at a time, just dying –
crying the first time I slept with a guy, not knowing why,
getting high, getting drunk, bingeing on junk food, a hunk I
screwed with a teeny penis, dense enough to call it immense
while stuffing tissues in his pants, the cancer that took my
father, his eyes at the end, his pain, my own when it claimed
him, the fact I blamed him for smoking, then took it up myself,
the act evoking only him, always grinning, the image unfailing,
unfading until now, along with how many others? So many.
Hearing the definition of rimming – ugh! – a fascination with
fallen women; Sylvia Plath, Joan of Arc, considering
martyrdom and doom in the dark of my room on the bed where
I lay with Billie Holiday on my player, offering up a prayer
when I thought I was pregnant, the succeeding bleeding that
proved I wasn't, a week in Morocco, a week in Prague, the
former a drag, the latter a joy, no matter the boy I was with
showed what a shit he was by constantly pointing out my
flaws, our separation, a weight fixation, a brief bulimia
flirtation, in bed with my mother that time with the cream and
the cheeses and peaches – Jesus – watching *Beaches*, being
held by her, how difficult it was to deny her after, the several
years alone, my bitterness honed, loneliness and mistrust
destroying lust, turning desire to dust and me to a shell until,
halfway to Hell, it was reignited by a slighted soul who
somehow stole my heart…

The sorry tale from start to finish, the joys, the pains, all
deleted, and what remains like the melody of a song, its lyrics
gone, and then, the theft of what's left, the tune, and soon the

pruning of thought itself, and I try to reclaim my waning name
in vain – it's gone – or where I'm from – that too – the who
and the why, the I; all fly from my mind till I just kind of am,
then…

Bam!

…a rent in my sunless sphere appears, lets in a light that sears
my eyes, I shut them tight and feel myself lifted from hot to
cold, enfolded in something soft and borne aloft, the waft of
many smells assailing me, the ability to identify them failing
me; the wind, the clamour, hammering in my ears, this fearsome
fusion of sounds into which I've been cast and to which, at last,
I open my eyes to see, through the glare, the face of a woman,
streaked with tears – I'm back in the world, it appears – and,
she's smiling down at me like you would at a child, her
expression melancholy yet beguiled, and, though I don't know
her at all, she evokes in me such love, I bawl, appalled as I am
by the idea that she's about to abandon me, to disappear, a fear
borne out when after a minute she puts her mouth to my ear
and, in it, whispers words I'm unable to decode…

Light up on A.

A

You'll have to be strong from here.

B

…my language having eroded so. Then a kiss and, slowly, she
withdraws and because all lexicon is gone, I try in vain to give
voice, as she leaves me for ever…

Light up on C.

C

End of the line...

B

...to the word that's endured beyond any other...

C

...time's almost up...

B

...Mother.

Light down on A *and* B.

C

...and there's no point denying the fact that I'm fucked, though I've ducked my doom so long, I don't really feel wronged that it's now just about upon me. I take a Locket from my pocket, pop it, crack the coating, noting the fact that the honey tastes much sweeter now I'm teetering over the precipice.

But less of this observation; acceleration's what we need and, indeed, it's hard to believe the kind of speed this truck can achieve. And as she does a nifty hundred and fifty up the motorway, I note the day has nearly begun, the sun in its rise erasing night and lighting my route and that of those in pursuit, once four, now nine, now joined by a helicopter flying overhead.

It's been a dead-straight run so far, but, approaching Dublin, that run is marrred by an escalation of cars and shit, necessitating split-second steering, which, I fear, my recurring exhaustion is queering up and causing a couple of wrong decisions resulting in a collision or two.

Like at The Red Cow, when I plough into a car and tear off two
of its doors, or in Inchicore, when, avoiding a bus, I annihilate,
or just about, some traffic lights, and, heart in mouth and
knuckles white on the wheel, I peel ahead in a fever, totally
juiced, toward Heuston Station, where another collision sends a
taxi crashing off the bridge and into the Liffey, the driver still
steering as if he can prevent his descent – a splash – he can't –
then a dash up the quays, squeezing through gaps in traffic,
nudging cars aside when the space isn't wide enough, some of
them crashing badly – tough.

They'll be debating, I'd say, what had been motivating me this
day. 'Was it insanity? Possibly. Did he simply snap? Perhaps.'
Never copping to the fact, I suppose, that the acts only arose out
of the combination of isolation and an aspiration to sing well.
For that I fell and fall, and for all I did, I'll pay. But, hey: there's
highs and there's lows and that's the way it goes. We live on
luck and...

Jesus fuck! There's a bang and the truck gives a little jump and
I'm bumped against the dash and flash on what's just occurred: a
bird just stepped into the road, a pregnant girl, half-glimpsed
before I mowed her down. What the fuck was she doing? Man,
I'm accruing victims fast, though it's evident this last – and Shane
of course – were only accidents. That's my defence in any case.

Anyway. Back to the chase, my flight, which right now seems to
have ceased or at least eased off, my hounders having
floundered, all except the helicopter. They stopped for the girl,
it seems, which deems the time correct to elect to find the
loading bay for the Jervis Centre, which I do, drive up and
enter, slipping by the delivery guys, with ease, distracted as they
are by some chick without clothes, in the *Daily Star*, I suppose,
the *Sun*, one of those.

The place still closed, it's like a tomb, I observe, as I zoom and
swerve toward the staff elevator, step inside and, moments later,
step back out, pass through another door, which deposits me on
the second floor of the car park, where, right there and then, a
silver Merc is pulling in, a man in a pinstriped suit stepping out
who turns and shouts to find a knife at his throat, then gurgles a

bit, says, 'Shit!' as it's slit, and falls to the floor, and I get in his car, although not before I take his keys and his parking ticket, and pay the fee, then, making my way in the Merc to the exit gate, which, rising, allows me out to the street, I speculate on whether I might just have the fuckers beat.

Though, wary of tempting fate, I drive with care, deferring to the law, till, drawing away from the city centre, I relent to the need to pull in and scan the sky for the helicopter which I see continues to hover over the Jervis. Hah! And, no longer nervous, I split, the wheels emitting a squeal as I peel away, me shouting, 'Yay!' then, 'Hey!' as a bump on the roof makes me jump, then a second sound, like steel being ground and the sight of sunlight blasting against the dash through a gash in the roof which widens by degrees. And I'm seized by shock as the car now rocks and the steel continues to peel, revealing a creature which, despite its features, its form, composed as it is of a hundred thousand worms, its size, is someone I recognise: myself, or rather, my other half.

I have to laugh as I'm pulled through the rip in the roof, the hole torn by my soul, and borne aloft on wings of worms, bound in arms against which I squirm and turn away to see at the Merc below which whips and flips on its side and slides to a stop outside a hardware shop, and my soul and I continue up and at a certain height, descend toward a construction site and enter, alight on a crane in its centre, the arm, upon which, without harm, we land.

And my soul unhands me and brands me a traitor, which I neither debate nor deny, though I try to apologise for selling him, telling him I was weak and a fool and...

'Shut the fuck up,' he says.

'All right, cool.'

'Now take off all of your clothes,' he says, and if I refuse, I know I'll be made to. So fade to me in my altogether, the chilly weather shrinking my nethers. Cut to my soul, his folded arms unfolding.

'C'mere,' he says, now holding them out.

'Why?' I say, though I wanna shout, 'Fuck this!' step off the crane and just fall, don't play his game. But all my will can't still his call, its pull, my resistance null and void to his arms spread wide into which I step as something slips into my rectum, from thence to my colon, cajoling its way into my intestine, twisting and turning, wending and worming this way and that, its final destination unknown until I moan and unleash a hot regurgitation of all I ate at the petrol station, making way for the entrance into my mouth of his tail upon which I'm now impaled.

And how I failed to notice the enormous crowd now gathered below, I don't know. Astonished, they gape as I'm punished, my public rape concluded with a smile, a kiss on the lips, 'You ready?' he says, then this: he lifts me above his head and, as I scream, arms and legs flaying, he tosses me off the crane and, once I fall to a certain height, the tail, still in my throat, grabs tight and my weight pulls my innards inside out till I'm suspended, swinging about on a length of intestine, a little less than dignified, you'll agree, looking up to see him grinning widely, having tied my entrails to the crane.

But the pain, so strong till now, as I look back down at the throng, is somehow subsumed as I'm consumed by the yen to sing. So, clearing my throat, I try a note or two and find my voice is strong and true and resounding, though, more astounding is the fact that I'm not bound up like before by shyness And, why? The enormous shame, I'd speculate, that my present state creates, its magnitude, negates any lesser humiliation.

So, filled with exhilaration at the gift of the weight that's been lifted this late, after waiting so fucking long, I launch into song and the crowd all start to sway, I swear, this way then that, all unaware of anything but the disembowelled man who swings, the song he sings, Bette Midler's 'Wind Beneath My Wings'. And, they're mesmerised – man, look at their eyes! – enraptured, captured, enchanted, transplanted by my voice to a better place, and I rejoice at the hour of my death that I'm getting to show them what I've got.

And yet.

The one who seems most moved of all is my soul. See him holding himself, the tears that seep as he weeps and run down his cheeks as if he's lamenting a loss.

I stop the song, perplexed, until he directs me to carry on. And I suspect from the look he gives me, his expression, that he forgives me my transgression, or at least understands now he's ascertained exactly what I stood to gain: its power, its splendour.

'Go on,' he says, with a tender smile and, momentarily reconciled to him, I recommence, the crowd again entranced by my supreme interpretation, peerless; fearless, even as I hit that final impossible section – you know it, I'm sure – the notes so pure, so high, the repetition of the lyric 'Fly', which most performers, not including Bette, just fail to get. They try to nail it by wailing it out or just shouting, flouting the fact that they lack what it takes, the fakes, which makes my execution, consummate as it is, the biz, and the buzz as I come to the end and a hush descends, a pause, then a frenzied reaction; cheers and applause that send up an awesome reverberation like thunder, carrying with it a combination of adoration and wonder, is such that I'm overwhelmed with exultation, but also stunned by the realisation that what I've just done is, without question, worth what's to come, and, in addition to this, that its bliss-inducing memory will be sure, you see, to ease whatever suffering is in store for me when I enter into Hell…

Lights up on A and B.

…I mean, I've heard tell that even the Devil remembered Heaven after he fell…

Blackout.

The End.

A Nick Hern Book

Terminus first published in Great Britain in 2007 as a paperback original by Nick Hern Books Limited, 14 Larden Road, London W3 7ST

This revised edition published in 2011, in association with the Abbey Theatre, Dublin

Terminus copyright © 2007, 2011 Mark O'Rowe

Mark O'Rowe has asserted his moral right to be identified as the author of this work

Cover image copyright © Ros Kavanagh
Cover design by Ned Hoste, 2H

Typeset by Nick Hern Books
Printed in Great Britain by CPI Bookmarque, Croydon, Surrey

A CIP catalogue record for this book is available from the British Library

ISBN 978 1 84842 174 5

Mixed Sources
Product group from well-managed forests and other controlled sources
www.fsc.org Cert no. TT-COC-002227
© 1996 Forest Stewardship Council
FSC